Joyful Play

with Toddlers

Recipes for Fun with Odds and Ends

Tools for Everyday Parenting Series

Sandi Dexter

Illustrated by Karen Pew

Parenting Press, Inc.
Seattle, Washington

Please note: Supervise children carefully and take responsibility for their safety. Parenting Press, Inc. assumes no liability for accident or injury resulting from use of the ideas suggested in this book.

Copyright © 1995 by Sandi Dexter
Illustrations copyright © 1995 by Parenting Press, Inc.
First edition, First printing

Printed in the United States of America

ISBN 1-884734-00-6 Paperback
ISBN 1-884734-01-4 Library binding

Cover and interior design by Cameron Mason
Cover illustration by Karen Anne Pew

Library of Congress Cataloguing-in-Publication Data
Dexter, Sandi, 1946–
    Joyful play with toddlers : recipes for fun with odds and ends / Sandi Dexter : illustrated by Karen Pew
        p.   cm. -- (Tools for everyday parenting series)
    ISBN 1-884734-01-4. -- ISBN 1-884734-00-6 (pbk.)
    1. Creative activities and seat work.   2. Toddlers--Recreation.   3. Play.   I. Pew, Karen.   II. Title.
III. Title: Joyful play.   IV. Series.
    GV1203.D47   1994
    790.1'922--dc20   94-23010
                                                                          CIP

Parenting Press, Inc.
P.O. Box 75267
Seattle, Washington 98125

Contents

About This Book

*J*oyful Play with Toddlers gives you ideas for turning everyday things into toys. Toddlers are curious about even the most ordinary objects. Watch your child as she handles something. You will be amazed at how much pleasure common things give her. She will teach you to look at everything in new ways. You will discover that an egg carton can do much more than hold eggs!

At around age 18 months to three years, your child is very busy learning to think and feel. She is also learning to tell the **difference** between thinking and feeling. This is the age when she starts to separate from her parents, too. You'll probably hear your toddler say "no" often, even when she doesn't really mean it.

Life with a toddler is easier when you understand your child and know what to expect. You can help her make the most of these intense two years by offering her lots of interesting things to do. Play and learning do not require lots of money.

Joyful Play with Toddlers begins with ideas to help you gain skills in parenting your growing child. The middle of the book has many ideas for play and learning. Some of these ideas have been put together in "Play Group Planning" to help you entertain small groups of toddlers on special occasions.

How Toddlers Learn

You are the most important teacher your child will ever have. When your child was a baby, she saw herself as part of you. As she enters toddlerhood, however, she begins to see herself as an individual. She is different from you. What you help her learn about herself will give her the confidence to move ahead.

Children watch and learn by copying what they see others doing. Sometimes they act out their own experiences with a stuffed animal or doll. For example, if you read to your toddler, you may see her reading to her teddy bear. If you fix things around the house or work on your car, you may see her copying you, using toys as tools.

Your child looks to you for guidance, and for love and comfort. She expects you to keep her safe. She is active and curious about everything. **Watch her all the time** so that she does not get hurt while she is exploring.

Toddlers are explorers

Toddlers are discovering what things are and exploring how they work. They learn through their senses. They look at objects from every side. They rattle, bang, touch, and taste as they explore. They do the same thing over and over again. Be sure to give your child time to learn and feel successful. For example, let your toddler put something into a box and take it out 27 times if she wishes.

Children like to play with ordinary things. These don't have to be new. They don't have to be called "toys" by a manufacturer. Everything is interesting. Instead of throwing away things you can't use anymore, give them to your child to play with. Make sure they are safe first.

Joyful Play with Toddlers tells you how to make toys from things you already have. It tells you where to get many things free or at low cost. You don't need a lot of money. You just need to look at throwaways as if you were a toddler.

Safety comes first

Take a walk through each room in your home. Make a note of things that could be dangerous. Some are obvious, some are not. Do these things to make your home safer for your toddler:

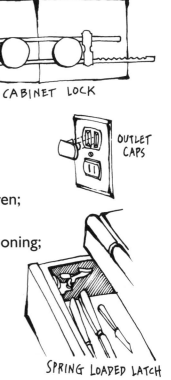

CABINET LOCK

OUTLET CAPS

- Put safety caps on electrical outlets;
- Put latches on cupboard doors;
- Lock up your medicine cabinet;
- Check for poisonous houseplants;
- Move household cleansers out of toddler's reach;
- Read the labels of nonfood items to see if they are safe for children;
- Ask your child's doctor for brochures on child safety;
- Buy a bottle of Syrup of Ipecac to induce vomiting in case of poisoning;
- Post emergency numbers by your telephone—
  - nearest neighbor,
  - pediatrician, hospital, or health care center,
  - poison control center,
  - police and fire stations,
  - your address, telephone number, and nearest cross streets.

SPRING LOADED LATCH

Remember, too, that people visiting may bring unsafe items with them. Ask friends to put their purses or bags in a closet that your child is unable to open. If you have overnight guests, ask them to keep cosmetic bags and make-up kits locked in their suitcases. Tell them you are looking out for your child's safety, as well as the safety of their belongings.

Before you give anything to your child to play with, check to see that it is safe. Here is an easy test for size: an object that fits inside a camera film canister or a small pill bottle is too small for a child who puts things in her mouth.

Some items do not make good toys:

- Styrofoam packing material, cups and plates, etc. are dangerous for children. If eaten, Styrofoam cannot be digested and is difficult to see by X-ray.
- Plastic bags or wrapping used to store food or toys can cause choking or suffocation. Use waxed bags for food and small boxes or cloth bags for toys.
- Small buttons, coins, marbles, small hard candies, or any toy which says it is not suitable for children under three are not safe. Check labels on toys and look carefully to see what your child can choke on if the toy comes apart.
- Anything tied around the neck could choke a child. Capes, necklaces, etc. should be worn only when you are closely supervising your child.

Anything left lying around is potentially dangerous to your curious explorer. After you have child-proofed your home, garage, and yard, you will relax and have a lot more fun with your toddler!

Be careful about offering food

Before you offer food to any child, ask the parent if there are any food restrictions. Some children may be allergic or unable to chew, swallow, digest, or may dislike a food. Some families have personal, religious, or cultural preferences about the food they eat, too.

As your toddler grows

Many children older than three years enjoy the activities in this book. Also, during times of change, such as being ill, starting school, or having a new sibling, children look to familiar things for comfort. Support your child's efforts to cope. Let him or her know it's okay to play again with toys that have been put aside.

Living with an Explorer

There may be times when you do not recognize that explorer as the sweet, easygoing person your child was. Where did he go? What makes him tick now?

Toddlers are learning to master their bodies and their feelings. They want to be independent. They insist on doing things themselves. Routine is important to them. The parenting tools listed here will help you cope with this new stage of development.

Look for good behavior

Children want and need attention from their parents. Your job will be easier if you look for behavior that you like and pay attention to it. Praise it and reward it. For example, say, "You used the potty and pulled your pants up all by yourself. Would you like a story now?"

Avoid problems

It is easier to avoid problems than to deal with them. Change things in the house: put breakables out of reach, put up baby gates, provide a low shelf or drawer full of unbreakable dishes in the kitchen, and so on.

Offer activities that are not too difficult for your child. This tells him, "I know that you are capable." Avoid trying to make your child hurry up. He will let you know when he is ready for new challenges.

Make your expectations clear. Be specific about what you want. Say, "We're going home now. You may walk to the car, or I will carry you."

Show your child positive ways to handle frustrating moments. Such coping skills will benefit him all his life, and make your life with him easier at this toddler stage.

Set reasonable limits

Because toddlers have not figured out how to manage their bodies or their feelings, they need you to set limits for them to keep them safe. They also will test your rules. Know ahead of time what you are willing to let your child try when you head to the park. If you know he is not able to go down the big slide alone, tell him ahead of time what he may do. Say, "Today you get to go down the wide slide. What else are you going to do at the park?" If he says, "Go down big slide," you can say, "You wish you could go down the big slide." You have acknowledged his feelings. Or you could offer him a choice by saying, "You can play on the swings or the merry-go-round. What will you try first?"

Giving limits to children offers them security. The child feels, "I know you won't let me hurt myself." Be sure to do what you say you will do. Your child thinks, "Mommy means what she says."

Acknowledge feelings

You can help your child gain skills in dealing with his emotions. Teach him words to use when he is frustrated to the point of tears. Get down on his level when you talk to him. Say, "I can see that you want to put that puzzle piece in and can't do it. Are you frustrated?" Or, "Your face tells me that you are sad you can't go with Daddy to the store."

Let him know you understand how he feels, even though you are not able to change things. Offer ideas for things he could do with those feelings. Give him experience in choosing options. "I'm sad [or angry] now. . . . I need to sit quietly [or do 10 jumping jacks]."

Remember that a toddler is not yet able to understand or look at things from another person's point of view. A toddler sees things only from his own point of view. He doesn't realize that if he bites another child, it will hurt that child. What he learns is, "If I bite him, he will cry."

Reduce power struggles

Limit the times you say "no" to your child by giving him opportunities to make his own choices. For example, say, "Today we are going outside to play. Do you want to wear your shorts or your swimsuit?" Or, "We have some time for snuggling. Do you want to sing some songs, or would you like me to read you a story? Do you want to choose the story from your book box, or shall I get one?"

Regain calm

There will be times when nothing seems to go right for your child. When that happens, you need to take a deep breath and spend a few minutes giving your complete attention to him. Sometimes that's all that is necessary to restore calm. Try reading your child's favorite story to him—more than once if he would like. Make up a song to go with the story. The words don't have to rhyme. Include your child's name in the song.

Try sitting in a rocking chair, or other comfortable place, and cuddle your toddler. He'll want to have his favorite snuggly blanket or toy. Often, five minutes spent quietly together will calm both of you.

If you don't feel calm yourself, you may find it hard to comfort your child. If that happens, have your child sit in his favorite place by himself. Tell him that you are going to sit in your favorite place, too, so that you can calm yourself. You may need only a moment to regain calm. You will also have shown your child a good way to deal with feelings of frustration or anger.

We have looked at ways to keep children safe and how to deal with emotions in safe, healthy ways. Now it's time to play!

Boxes and Boxes of Boxes

Boxes are great fun for children. They can become space ships, houses, trains, furniture, hiding places, wagons, . . . The possibilities are endless. The variety of sizes and shapes of boxes makes them ideal for imaginative play. Think about the different kinds of boxes you might have around the house:

shoe boxes	gift boxes	mailing boxes	appliance boxes
cereal boxes	tissue boxes	clothing boxes	storage boxes

Save them all. Now you have hours, days, and weeks of fun for your child.

Over and under, In and out

Toddlers enjoy crawling in and out of big boxes. Watch your child go in and out, around, up and down, and through the box. Use the opportunity to give her words for those actions:

"You're in the box."   "You're over the box."   "You're under the box."

Fill and dump

After a child has explored how he can use the big box to play in himself, he may use it as a container to fill and empty. The act of filling and emptying is what is important. Toddlers practice this over and over. A teddy bear, doll, or other favorite item can fit into a big box. Your child may like to carry small toys or objects around in boxes.

Give him a small box, like a shoe box. Put it down near his toys. He will probably take the lid off and begin loading things into the box.

Next, try cutting a few holes in the lid of the box. Show your child how some toys fit through the holes. When all the toys are inside the box, take the lid off and dump them out again. He'll love the noise and confusion of things falling out.

Variations using other containers:

Cut holes in the top of a large margarine container.

Use a coffee can with holes cut in the plastic lid.

Use an oatmeal container without the lid.

Pretend games with boxes

Around 18 months, your child begins to play "pretend" games. Boxes can become anything she might imagine. She will enjoy having her own make-believe stove, refrigerator, or washing machine and car, train, bus, or boat.

Box stove. Tape a box closed. Turn it on its side and draw four big circles on top to represent stove burners. Draw knobs on the side.

When your toddler loses interest in "cooking," cut an opening for the oven door. The stove has new appeal because she can "bake" all kinds of goodies. Toddlers love to put things in and out of boxes.

Box desk. Make a desk for your child with a sturdy box. Cut the box open on one side, so her legs can go underneath when she sits down in a chair or on another smaller, sturdy box.

Garages and buildings. Shoe boxes make great garages for cars, fire stations for rescue vehicles, houses for tiny teddy bears and dolls. They can be used for storage of these toys as well.

Train. Toddlers spend a lot of time going places with their parents. Your child enjoys pretending to "drive" her box. Even the youngest toddler enjoys this simple idea of how to use a box.

Hook several boxes together with ribbon or yarn to make a train. Your toddler enjoys watching the train cars swing as she pulls them across the floor. "Let's take teddy for a ride in the train," she might suggest.

Tip: When your child won't go to bed, suggest she hop into the train and ride into the bedroom. You can attach a short rope or belt to pull the train.

Box maze. Cut holes in the sides of boxes and put them together around the room. Show your child how to go in and out of the boxes. Encourage her with suggestions, "Let's see you climb through the boxes!"

Appliance box buildings. Look for boxes used to ship new stoves, dishwashers, washing machines, and dryers. Make a house, store, gas station, fast-food shop, hospital, or other familiar building from these sturdy, large boxes. They will last a long time and give your toddler many hours of happy imaginative play. They also provide space that is "just mine." You can get these boxes from appliance dealers.

Milk Cartons

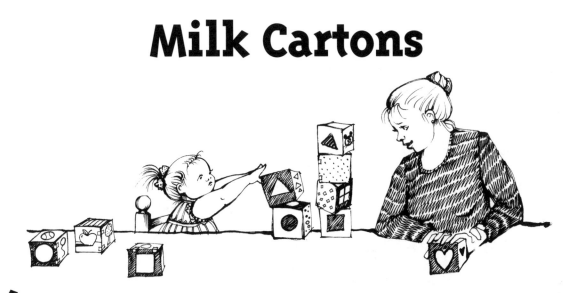

You can make blocks for your toddler out of the empty milk cartons you and your friends save. Both quart and half gallon sizes are useful.

Mark a cutting line on two cartons. Cut along the lines. Push one cube into the other so all sides are closed. Tape around the cut edges. You can cover blocks with different kinds of materials. You may have contact paper, construction paper, shiny paper, sandpaper, fabrics, wrapping paper, and other coverings around your home. Look for these and other inexpensive coverings at a variety store, hardware store, or fabric store.

Picture cubes

Glue photos of family members on each side of the cube. The photos will last longer if you cover them with clear contact paper, available at variety and hardware stores.

Guessing game with picture cube

Sit on the floor with your child and show her one side of the block. Ask her, "Is it Grandma?" or, "Whose picture is this?"
Tip: Before your child can talk, she can nod yes or no to your questions. You will be helping her learn words for familiar things in her world.

Variations on picture cubes. Cover each side of a cube with photos of familiar items from a magazine or catalog. If you want to surprise your toddler, use shiny, silver paper on one side of the cube. It acts as a mirror for your child's face.

Use construction paper to cover each side in a different color. You can play a color guessing game. Start by naming the colors for your child. Later ask her to name the colors for you. For example, "Can you find the purple side?" or, "What color do you like today?"

Block games

Help your child play with the blocks. For example, begin lining up the blocks end to end. Say, "Let's make a road for your cars," or, "Let's make a fence around your farm [or zoo or wild] animals." You can use the toys your child has in many ways.

Watch your child as she plays with the blocks. Toddlers begin building towers with one or two blocks. By age two they can balance six or more blocks on top of each other. When your child stacks blocks say, "You stacked that block on top of the other. Can you do that again?" Stacking is an important skill to learn and practice.

Cans and Lids

Cans make good toys. Save cans of different sizes. Check for sharp edges. Pinch down any sharp spots with a pliers. Then cover the edge of the can with cloth tape or duct tape.

Nesting cans

Give your toddler three cans of different sizes. Use small, medium, and large cans that will nest inside one another. Show her how the cans fit inside one another. At first, she may only be able to put the smallest can into the largest. As she practices she will be able to put the middle-sized cans into other cans. Give her time to do this over and over again.

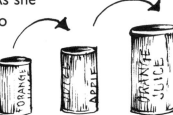

When she tires of putting three cans together, give her two or three more cans in between the largest and smallest sizes.

Can cone

Make a can cone by stacking a small can on top of a larger one. Give your child the smallest can to put on top of the cone. Take the cone apart and let her try to build one.

Too big, Too little, Just right

Find an object that just fits inside the medium-sized can. Let your toddler put it in the can and take it out. Ask her to put it in the small can. When it doesn't fit, say, "Too big." Repeat this game by putting the object in the big can and say, "Too little." Then try the medium-sized can again, saying, "Just right."

This game lets your child explore size relationships and gives her the words to describe different sizes.

Frozen juice can lids

Frozen juice can lids make good toys for even the youngest toddler. They have no sharp edges, are the right size for handling easily, and are shiny. Here are several ways to recycle lids into toys.

Slide 'em in a box. For this game you will use the box with the slots in its lid (see page 19). Give your toddler a stack of juice can lids. Show her how to fit one into the slot and watch it disappear into the box. Say, "Can you do that?" or, "I wonder where the lid went? Let's take the top off the box and see." Your child will have the most fun emptying the box to start the game all over.

Stack 'em tall. Fill a box or other container with juice can lids. Take out two lids and stack them. Give one lid to your child. Ask, "Can you put this one on top of the stack?" Count the lids as she puts them on the stack. She does not understand the concept of numbers yet, but delights in the rhythm of your counting. Soon she will be "counting" as she puts things together. It is all right if she mixes up numbers.

Face pennies. Cut out catalog or magazine pictures of faces. Glue them onto juice can lids. Put lids, face side down, on the floor. As your child picks each one up, say, "That is the baby," "That is the man," "That is the little girl," and so on. Ask your child to point to the nose, eyes, mouth, hair, and other objects in the pictures.

Variations on face pennies. Use pictures of familiar animals, such as birds, cats, dogs, ducks, and fish for an animal game that you play like the face game.

Decorate some lids with stickers and put magnetic tape on the back of the lid. Your child will enjoy playing with magnets on the surface of the refrigerator or on a cookie sheet.

Matching coins

For an older toddler (2 to 3 years old), you can make two of every decorated juice can lid and play a "matching" game. Start with three or four sets of matching pictures. You can slowly increase the number of matched sets as your child can concentrate longer. Place the sets of lids picture-side up on the floor or table. First, you pick up one picture and ask your child to pick up its match.

After she has learned to do this, you can ask her to hand you matched pairs or to put the pairs together. Say, "Can you give me the lids with the dog on them?" or, "Show me the two lids that have a dinosaur on them." Your toddler needs skills in seeing similarities for matching socks, shoes, and other objects. Later she needs these skills for reading and math.

Tip: Flower bulb catalogs have beautiful colored photographs of flowers. Ask your neighbors to save catalogs for you. Try to get two of the same catalog, so you will have two of each flower.

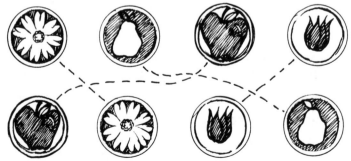

Puzzles

Homemade puzzles are fun to make. Best of all, you are not limited to the varieties you find in a store. Puzzles help toddlers and young children learn to see similarities and differences, a necessary first step to learning to read later on. Puzzles also help them with hand-eye coordination, a skill necessary for using tools, performing many activities, and eventually writing.

Single circle puzzle

Trace around a plate on the center of a piece of heavy cardboard. Cut out the circle with a sharp knife or single-edged razor blade. **(Don't use these tools around toddlers. Make these puzzles when children are asleep. Put the tools away in a safe place.)** Make the edges as smooth as possible. You now have a simple shape puzzle for your toddler. Show him how to take the circle piece out and put it back in again. Then give him the circle piece and ask him to put it in the puzzle.

Circles are the easiest shapes for young children to fit into a puzzle since they fit no matter which way the child puts them in.

Variations on the circle puzzle. When your child can do the puzzle with one circle, he is ready for a puzzle with several circles, **all the same size.** Your toddler needs lots of practice before you give him other shape puzzles to do.

Puzzles of other shapes. Make new puzzles with a square, a triangle, a rectangle, and so on. If he gets frustrated because he can't fit the new shape into the hole, give him the old circle puzzles. Try the new ones again several days later.

Simple picture puzzle

Around age two, your child can enjoy other simple puzzles. Make a puzzle using the front of the box of his favorite breakfast cereal. Cut that piece in two parts down the middle. Show your toddler how to put the two pieces together to complete the puzzle. Any kind of printed box can become a puzzle.

Photo puzzle

Glue a favorite photo of your child onto cardboard or other sturdy backing to make a puzzle of him! This is great fun for toddlers.

You can make puzzles from other familiar items, like labels from canned fruit or pictures from an old calendar or magazine. Be sure to glue them on cardboard before you cut them into shapes. The easiest shape for your toddler to put together will be a square or rectangle cut in half. After he masters a two-piece puzzle, you can make puzzles with three or four shapes.

Books

A younger toddler can "read" by flipping quickly through a book without reading the words. If he points to a picture you can give the name for it. This helps him learn words to name things. Say, "That is a pig and pigs say 'oink, oink.'" Move on to the next page he wants to look at. Go as fast or as slowly as he wants.

As your child can sit still and do the same activity longer, spend more time looking at books. Think about your child and what you are looking at, not about chores you need to do. You will both enjoy this pleasurable, relaxed time. Your toddler will learn many skills and gain lots of information from this activity.

Let him curl up on your lap as he looks at the pictures. The sound of your voice teaches him the rhythm of language even when he doesn't understand all the words you say. He learns to think about "what happens next" as you (or he) turn the pages.

How to choose a book for a toddler

The young toddler recognizes objects more easily in clear photographs than in drawings. Sturdy books or cardboard ("board") books are easier to handle by those chubby little fingers. Rhyming books teach children the beauty of language and appeal to their sense of rhythm. Look for books that have short rhymes. Toddlers learn to look for what is the same or different in pictures. Pointing to pictures and turning pages helps develop small muscle coordination.

At first, pick books with lots of pictures and few words. As your child grows, she enjoys longer stories, and you can read books with more words. Choose books you like. Young children like to hear the same story over and over again! You'll want to be reading something you like, too.

You can borrow books at the library, ask friends and relatives to pass on books their children don't need, or buy used books in bookstores, thrift stores, and at garage sales. You can also make books for your child.

"My book!"

A book especially made by you and your child is a very personal item to her. Look through magazines and cut out pictures she likes. Glue the pictures on cardboard and use yarn to tie the pages together. An old three-ring binder makes a good book holder, too. You can paste a favorite picture on the cover. She will be delighted with a book of pictures she chooses herself.

You can make the book even more personal with family photographs. Begin with a picture of your child as a baby and then a recent photograph of her. Take a picture of her doing something she especially enjoys. Put in photos of family members and pets, her room, and familiar objects.

To make these books sturdy and water resistant, put the pages inside plastic bags of the same size. Sew several "pages" of the bags together on the "zipped" side. The book can go almost anywhere with your child.

Safety note: If the plastic bag tears, repair it with clear tape or remove that page.

Tip: This kind of book is comforting to a child away from home because it reminds her of familiar things. It also helps her when a family member is away. You can let your child know you understand that she misses someone. You can help her talk about her feelings. Say, "I know you miss Grandma. This picture of her reminds you that she loves you and misses you too when she is away."

Busy books

You can very easily make your own busy book like those expensive ones you see in the stores. Use sturdy squares of felt fabric for the "pages." Sew or glue items onto the felt. Here are some ideas for pages you can make:

PEEK A BOO!

- Put a picture of your child into a plastic bag and sew that onto the felt. Cover the bag with a piece of cloth to make a peek-a-boo page.
- Glue a fake-fur remnant onto the felt page and follow it with other texture pages such as sandpaper, velvety wallpaper, corduroy fabric, ridged cardboard, plastic bubble packing wrap, and other interesting textures.
- Sew buttons securely onto a felt page. Use a variety of sizes and shapes. Be sure to check frequently that buttons are secure.
- Sew fabric ribbon pieces onto a felt page. Your child will enjoy the flutter of the ribbons as well as the different colors and designs. (Check your local fabric shop for ribbon remnants.)

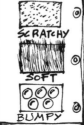

SCRATCHY
SOFT
BUMPY

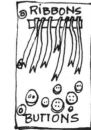

RIBBONS
BUTTONS

POLK·A·DOTS
STRAIGHT LINES
WIGGLY LINES

Mirrors

Toddlers love to look at themselves in the mirror. They are not at all self-conscious and take great delight in spending long periods looking at themselves. This activity increases their self-awareness and self-esteem.

Safety note: Give your child a mirror made of a **nonbreakable material** like acrylic or metal to play with.

Mirror mimic game

Sit with your child on your lap in front of a mirror. Wave to your child. Does he wave back? Make other motions to see if he imitates you. Imitate your child's facial expressions. Does he notice?

If so, copy his expression and do this until he tires of this game. If he doesn't notice you imitating him, say, "I see your happy face. Do you see mine?"

Point to your nose, ears, chin, etc. and ask your child to point to the same on his face. Make up a song about putting your finger on your nose, your hand on your head, your finger near your eye, and so on.

Happy, sad, scared, and mad faces

Children need to learn about feelings. They also need to learn words for what they feel. You can show your toddler feelings and tell him the words that go with them. You can talk about other people's feelings and help your child say what he thinks they feel. For example, "That girl is crying. She feels unhappy."

Ask him to show you a happy face and then you show him your happy face. Repeat this game with many different feelings. Ask him to look in the mirror and make the faces you suggest. Say, "Can you make a silly face? Oh my, you look so silly."

If your child doesn't yet know how to make a face when you ask, then you make the face for him. You can say, "This is how I look when I am scared. Can you make a face like mine?"

Make up a story using several "feeling" words and ask your child to show you how he would look feeling different ways. Young children can express happy and sad. Later they will learn to express other feelings that you name.

Tip: Giving children words for a wide variety of feelings helps them learn how recognize and express those feelings. Remember that feelings are neither good nor bad. They just are.

Sock Toys

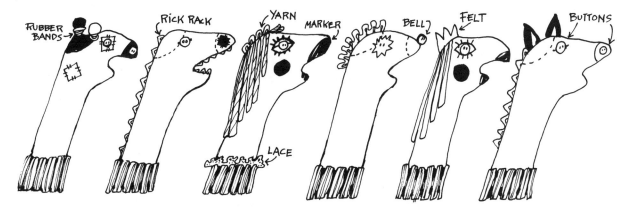

RUBBER BANDS→   RICK RACK   YARN   MARKER   BELL   FELT   BUTTONS   LACE

Have you ever thought of socks as toys? You can surprise your child with sock games and toys. Such an unexpected use of socks is fun for an ill child who needs a distraction or for a child who is fussy or out of sorts.

Snakes

Knee-high tube socks make great soft snakes. With a permanent marker, make two eyes and a mouth at the toe end. A smiling face will spark one from a frowning child. Stuff the sock with a rolled hand towel. You can sew the open end closed, or leave it open. When you remove the towel, your snake becomes a hand puppet! If you use a white sock, your child can color the snake with water-soluble markers.

Puppets

Your hand inside a short sock transforms it magically into a creature with a mouth. It can talk in a high, squeaky voice or a low, jolly tone. Add eyes with a permanent marker and, if you like, add lengths of yarn at the end of the sock's toe for hair. Your child might like to help you decorate the body of the sock. Sock puppets can do anything and be anything, so use your imagination and have fun with your toddler.

PULL THE SOCK OVER YOUR HAND AND THE HEEL OVER YOUR KNUCKLE

Dolls

Make a doll from a sock and a receiving blanket or hand towel. Stuff the toe into the heel of the sock to form a ball, leaving only about five inches of the open end free. Then, holding the open end, wrap the blanket around the head to make a scarf and then several times around the free end to make the baby's body. These soft babies are great for emergencies and can safely go to bed with your child.

Dolls are important toys for both girls and boys because they allow children to take care of something the way their parents take care of them. Dolls are also comforting toys for small children.

Fun in the Kitchen

Children love to be where you are. But they are often underfoot just when you need to move around quickly. Here are some safe and fun things for your child to do while you work in the kitchen.

Kitchen toys

Sometimes the drawer where you store all your plastic containers holds more fascination for your toddler than the most expensive toy. The items in the drawer have no specific purpose as far as your child is concerned. They can do everything.

Mixing bowls and measuring cups. Different sizes of bowls and cups fit inside one another. Your toddler will nest them together. Maybe he will turn them over to see what happens. You can say, "Oh, the big bowl covered the small bowl," or, "Where did the small bowl go? Oh, there it is!"

Give him plastic measuring cups. Let him discover that one fits inside another. It will take a while to get the sequence right, big to small. For now, the little one goes easily into the big one. After he masters nesting the cups, you can turn them over and say, "Can you put the small one on top of the big one, like this?"

Kitchen gadgets. These fascinate toddlers. The shapes, materials they are made of, and the uses for them are all interesting. Let your child use his imagination in how he would like to play with safe gadgets. Your whisk might become a stringed instrument as he plucks and pulls one of the wires and lets go. "Wow, look at those

wires wiggle!" you might say to him. Two wooden spoons make great drumsticks. Give him a metal bowl, a frying pan, or let him bang on the floor. Rolling pins are fun to roll across the floor, too.

If you are going to be busy cooking, give your child your smallest bowl, a mixing spoon, measuring cup, and a saucepan. As you talk about fixing dinner, your child likes to imitate you.

Toddlers love what is familiar to them. They like to play with toys that represent home and family. Let yours help with real situations like putting the napkins on the table, sponging off the chairs before dinner, and sweeping up after dinner. He will feel a sense of accomplishment. You are beginning to teach responsibility in a low-key way.

Cooking up some fun

One of the most enjoyable toys you can make for your child is a batch of playdough. Playdough gives hours and hours of creative play to your child (and you). Make sure your toddler understands that playdough is not to eat, but to play with!

Recipe for best-ever playdough

In a saucepan, combine:
1 cup flour
1/2 cup salt
2 tablespoons cream of tartar
Add to the flour mixture:
1 cup cold water with
a few drops of food coloring
1 tablespoon vegetable oil

Mix ingredients with a whisk to remove lumps. Cook over medium heat, stirring frequently with a wooden spoon. Mixture will begin to stick to the sides and bottom of the pan. Keep stirring until it sticks together and no longer looks slimy.

Turn mixture out onto counter and knead 10 times. When it is cool, your child can play with it. Store the playdough in a covered container so that it doesn't dry out. It doesn't need to be refrigerated and will keep indefinitely.

Variations. Try adding a drop or two of flavoring to the water mixture to give the playdough a pleasant aroma. Be sure to do this **after** your child has passed the stage of putting everything in his mouth, or the scent will tempt him to taste it.

Instead of food coloring, add one tablespoon of nonmetallic confetti dots to the flour mixture. You can call this variation celebration playdough, magic playdough, or stardust playdough. The confetti will appear as your toddler plays. **Safety note:** Glitter is not safe to use around toddlers. The sharp edges can cause eye injury.

Poke, pat, and pound

First, let your child hold the playdough to feel the weight. Say, "It's heavy, isn't it! Let's put it on the table. Can you poke it with your finger, like this?" Let him explore the texture and other features of the playdough. Does it leave a hole if he sticks his finger in it? Will it stick to his finger? What will happen if he grabs a bit of it? Will it fall apart? Give your child lots of time to explore the playdough by poking, patting, and playing.

Playdough pancake

Get out your rolling pin and let your child flatten the playdough. He will take great delight in watching the shape change from a rounded ball to a giant pancake. Show him how to poke "designs" on the pancake.

Kooky cookies

After he has had lots of time to explore the wonders of flattening the playdough with the rolling pin, give him cookie cutters. Now your toddler can make playdough cookies to put in that make-believe kitchen oven you made from a box.

Kitchen wizards

Many kitchen utensils are fun to use with playdough. Test them yourself first to make sure they are safe. Try these: potato masher, slotted spoon, pizza cutter (not too sharp), and garlic press. Other useful items are a play dish set, small muffin tin, small cookie sheet, and spatula. Children like to imitate what they see you doing, so these familiar items have great appeal. By using these tools in play, your toddler is learning how he'll use them in real cooking someday.

Porcupine playdough

Your child can use flat, wooden sticks with the playdough to make imaginative sculptures. On his own, he may discover that the sticks can become legs or buildings or trees or. . . .

Older toddlers will be able to use toothpicks instead of flat sticks, but don't forget to **show him** the sharp points on the toothpicks.

Tip: Check in your neighborhood thrift store for other unusual items to use with playdough. Look for individual, metal gelatin molds, small tart pans, and plastic containers in interesting shapes.

Water, Water Everywhere

Think about how relaxing a long, warm bath can be. Children can enjoy the fun of playing with water without getting in the tub. You need a plastic dishpan, a small table, and plenty of towels. If you have a dishwasher, put the dishpan of water and toys on the open dishwasher door. That way most of the water should go into the dishwasher and not onto the floor.

Safety note: Watch for spills. Wet floors are dangerous!

Many items are fun to use in water play:

- Measuring cups and spoons are ideal for water play. They vary in size and there are enough of them for the child to stay interested, filling and emptying each one many times.

- Small plastic bottles are nice. It doesn't take much water to fill them, so there's not much water for spilling. As your toddler gets older, use a permanent marker and draw lines at various levels on the outside of the bottles. Show your toddler how to fill the bottle to the water line. This teaches good eye-hand coordination and encourages problem solving.

- Shaving cream caps are just right for your toddler's small hands. Instead of throwing away the caps from your hair spray, shaving cream, shampoo, deodorant, and other containers, consider them for possible use with water play.

- Yogurt, margarine, and jam containers are good for water play. Poke holes in the bottoms of some containers and let your child discover the water trickling out. Vary the number of holes so that different amounts of water leak out.

- Funnels are great fun for toddlers. They are fascinated to see the water come pouring out the bottom. The funnel never fills up! Funnels can be used to help fill cups and bottles.

- Large plastic pop (soda) bottles are great because you get two toys in one. Cut off the top portion of the pop bottle to make a funnel. Cut again near the bottom to make a cup. These also work well outside in the sandbox and are easily replaced when they break or get squashed. Make sure to smooth the edges.
- Sponges are fascinating. Cut up one of your kitchen sponges and let it dry out. Show your toddler how the sponge changes when you put it in the water. The color darkens and the sponge grows larger. When all the sponge pieces are wet, show her how to squeeze the water out of them (over the dishpan).

Bubbles
Recipe for billions of bubbles

Mix together gently:

1 gallon water

1/2 cup Dawn® detergent

2 tablespoons glycerin (get at the drug store)

This activity works very well on rainy or damp days. The bubbles like wet air. Let your child make bubbles by stirring the water around. Older toddlers will delight in using a whisk or hand-held egg beater to make more and more bubbles.

Ocean blue

Put a drop of blue food color into a pan of water. Now you have a tiny lake for your child's boats to sail on.

For a change, let her play with dried beans, rice, or oatmeal poured into a dishpan, instead of water. She will enjoy the different textures and colors.

Tip: Playing in water or other substance is a great sensory experience for your child. Touch helps your child's brain develop and gives her a chance to explore the world in small ways. Pouring, dumping, and measuring are all important tasks for her. These activities help her develop eye-hand coordination, as well as control over both small and big muscles.

Make-Believe Story Boxes

You can provide wonderful hours of play for your child by putting together make-believe story boxes. Here are a few ideas, using lots of things you may have around the house. If you need or want more items in a story box, visit a thrift shop or yard sale, or ask friends or neighbors to keep these items in mind when they are housecleaning.

Toddlers like to recreate experiences they have had personally when they play. Another way to introduce them to adventures is by reading stories to them. Books can give you more ideas for new make-believe story boxes to make.

Creation crate

This box contains art materials. Your child may already have a lot of these, but some of the suggestions may be new. Into a suitable box, put any or all of the following supplies:

computer paper
chunky crayons
strips of sticky dot labels
stickers
watercolor markers
(kids love the bold or fluorescent colors)
pieces of wrapping paper
tape of all kinds
glue sticks
picture fronts from greeting cards
pictures from old calendars and magazines
5 x 7 index cards
pieces of yarn and string
paper plates

Camping kit

You can create the outdoors in the house. All you need are a few things to help your toddler's imagination along. A sheet or blanket placed over a table makes a great tent. Add the following items and send your child "camping":

sleeping bag
(a pillowcase will work)
small pots and pans
red and orange construction paper
or tissue paper wadded up ("fire")
backpacks made from folded paper
    grocery sacks
storybook about camping
list of songs to sing around the "campfire"
flashlight, the most popular item

Cleaning day

Children love this activity. Put together a cleaning bucket, with a dusting rag, a small sponge, and a scrubber or scrub brush. Put a small amount of water in the bottom of the bucket. Let your child help clean by washing down the cupboard doors or dusting those hard-to-reach areas like table and chair legs.

Let's play house

Because a toddler's world centers around his home, he loves to imitate what he sees happening there. Items to go in this box include some discarded clothing, such as a shirt or two, scarves, handbags, hats, shoes, etc. Use plastic containers for child-sized bowls, the plastic lids for plates and provide some plastic forks and spoons. Add a piece of fabric for a tablecloth. Old, nonworking, small household appliances, such as a broken camera, small portable radio, or other safe item will add to the fun. Your child's imagination can easily supply details to make up for what is missing or not working.

Scarf Magic

Your child's imagination can make scarves into many different things. Ask relatives and friends for scarves and check thrift stores and garage sales. Try to build up a good supply.

Dancing scarves

Even the youngest toddler will enjoy dancing with scarves. Make sure they are not so long that she trips on them. If any scarf is too big, just tie a knot in the middle. The knot makes a convenient handle. Dancing with scarves is great fun! It can be a quiet activity, too. Turn the radio to the classical music station or other station playing calm music to set the tone for slow, quiet, soft motions.

Magic land

You can create a magical place for your toddler with scarves. Together, you and she can drape a scarf over the backs of two chairs to make a soft, colorful ceiling for a hideaway. Use tape to attach the scarf to the chairs, if necessary. Tie several scarves together and wind them around three table legs for a tent-like house for your child.

Amazing scarves

Dangle lots of scarves with their corners taped to the edges of a card table. This makes a soft screen for your child to play behind. She'll enjoy going through the scarves to get under the table.

Scarf costumes

Tie two scarves together at two corners. Slip your toddler's head through the hole so the scarves hang from her back and her chest. Wrap a larger scarf around your child's waist as a belt. Will she be a star traveller? Or a robot? She will probably surprise you.

Make wings by rolling a scarf into a tube. Put a rubber band around the middle. Unroll the two ends and you have . . . wings! Tie the wings to your child with another scarf slipped through the rubber band. **Safety note:** Anything tied around the neck can choke a child. A child playing with scarves must be closely supervised. Put scarves away in a safe place when the activity is finished.

Singing and Dancing

Singing helps young children build many skills. When children sing they learn to listen and express themselves in new ways. They learn about rhythm and beat, and develop new vocabulary. They hear beauty and feel the joy of using their own voices.

You can share the pleasure of songs you remember from your own childhood. Sing while you work or play with your child to convey your happiness. Sing lullabies to soothe and relax your child and make bedtimes happy. If you don't remember any songs, borrow a songbook from the library and learn some songs you like. If you feel you really can't carry a tune, chant the words to songs and poems in a rhythmical way. Children are not critical of a singer's ability. They will love whatever you can do.

Make a list of all the nursery rhymes, camp songs, hymns, folk songs, and popular songs you know. It's easy to forget how many you know and get stuck singing the same songs over and over. Your child may request a favorite song, however, until you are tired of it. Take a deep breath, and sing it again. Repetition is important.

Personal songs

Almost any song you sing to your child can be personalized by changing the words just a little. Instead of, "There was a farmer, had a dog," sing, "Young John Aaron had a cat and Chrissie was her name-o." In the "Wheels on the Bus" song, add verses to use your child's name: "We're sitting by the window and Nina's looking out, Nina's looking out." We give our children a powerful message about our love for them when we put their names to music.

"I See It!" songs

While you are driving in the car, walking down the street, or waiting for the bus, sing about things you and your child see. If your child comments on something he sees, try to make up a song or chant about it.

Radio, records, compact discs, tapes

Children love music. Eventually you will get tired of singing the day away. When you or your toddler needs a change, turn on the radio. You will find a wide selection of musical styles, from classical to ethnic folk music. It is good for your child to hear variety in music. If you have a turntable and old records, your toddler will enjoy seeing how the machine works, as well as listening to the music. Look for compact discs and tapes of children's music at garage sales and in thrift stores.

May I have this dance?

Even though toddlers can get about on their own, they still enjoy being held. Put some slow, rhythmic music on and dance with your child. A child who would rather walk than be held will still let you hold him while you are dancing. If he gets wiggly, put him down and dance together.

Variation. Play fast music and boogie with your child. His face will tell you if he enjoys it. Give your child a bell or rattle to accompany the music he hears. Show him how to put the bell up high, down low, on his knee, on his toe. Make motions to the music. Don't expect your toddler to keep time with the music. He is gaining awareness of the beat. Keeping time to it comes later.

Dancing props

Use scarves to add drama to the dancing. Use words like "swish" and "float" to put language to the movements he sees the scarves make. Cut the centers out of plastic-dish lids and tie ribbons on the ring for streamers. Your child can grasp the ring easily, or he can put it on his wrist and move his arms as he dances. You can make dance wands by wrapping paper strips or strips of ribbon around paper-towel tubes.

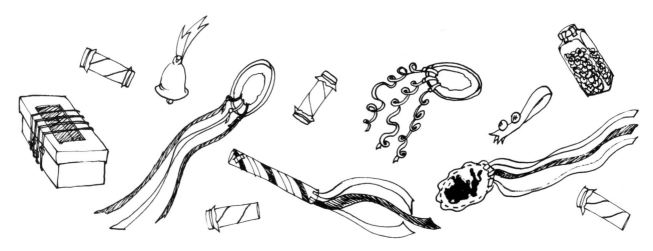

Mirror dancing

Dance in front of a mirror without a prop. Suggest to your child that he dance up high—show him how to stretch his arms and neck by saying, "Can you point your head up to the sky? What about your arms and fingers, can they touch the ceiling?" Move to a low level by asking your child to crouch down like a cat. Say, "Look at that cat in the mirror, can the cat stretch his leg out to the side?" Do the same actions as your child to reinforce what he is doing.

Tip: Dancing offers a way for children to gain awareness and control of their bodies. It is a wonderful outlet for self-expression. It is also a creative and positive way to use that seemingly boundless energy.

Kitchen Band

Children love noise! They love to hear what happens when you bang a spoon on a pot, shake an object, or knock things together. Homemade "instruments" can provide fun when you and your toddler make them and when you create music with them.

Tambourines

Start with two small paper plates. Let your child decorate the bottoms with markers and draw designs or glue scraps of paper or ribbon to the plates. Put some large pebbles or dry beans inside one plate. Cover that with the other plate and staple the two together. Make sure there are no gaps at the edges of the plate where beans, etc. could fall out. Give the tambourine to your child and let him shake and bang to his heart's content.

You need beans, a stapler with staples and paper plates.

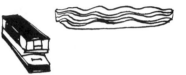

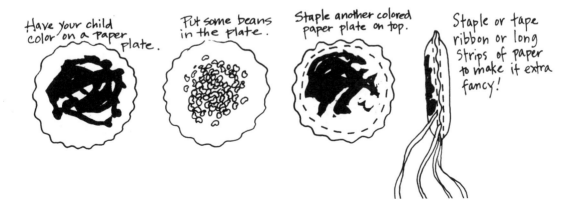

Have your child color on a paper plate.

Put some beans in the plate.

Staple another colored paper plate on top.

Staple or tape ribbon or long strips of paper to make it extra fancy!

Rubber band banjo

Cut a hole about 3 x 3 inches in the lid of a shoe box. Cut notches in each end of the lid and put the lid on the box. Stretch rubber bands over the whole box lengthwise. Tape them to the box on both ends so they don't slip off. Your child can strum or pluck the rubber bands to make different sounds. Sing along to the music he makes.

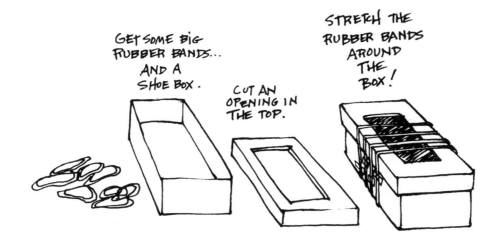

Silly shakers

You can make lots of different kinds of shakers for your toddler. Look around the kitchen for an empty plastic juice bottle, a small juice can, or a film canister. Fill the container you choose with dried beans, uncooked rice, dried peas, a few pennies, a key, a safety pin, or any other item. Tape the opening or lid shut. Now you are both ready to shake a leg!

FILL PLASTIC JUICE BOTTLE WITH BEANS! (Tape it Shut.)

More instruments

A cake rack with a string attached can be a homemade "triangle." Give your toddler a spoon to hit it with. Make toilet-paper tube kazoos by attaching waxed paper to one end of the tube with a rubber band. Hum into the other end. Empty, round oatmeal boxes with lids and wooden spoons make great drums and drumsticks. Use your imagination, experiment a little, and you'll find more instruments in your kitchen. It is amazing how many items can produce unusual sounds that delight your toddler.

• KAZOO... (WAX PAPER ON TOILET PAPER ROLL.)

• TOILET PAPER ROLL SHAKER

Art of Creation

The magic of creating is something that people of all ages find appealing. Even the youngest toddler enjoys drawing and painting. These activities give your child a chance to be independent. Watch your toddler as she explores the wonder of putting a crayon to paper and moving it around. Say to her, "See the line squiggling across the paper where the crayon just went!"

Set up a special place where your child can work. Make a small easel from a cardboard box. Cut off the top and bottom and one side of the box. Pull two ends together until they just touch and tape them together to make a triangle shape. Put the widest part down as the base and you have an easel. Use tape to hold paper in place. Put an old towel or a piece of plastic or old shower curtain beneath it. Your child is ready to paint.

Here are some items you will want to have on hand for your artist:

For the young toddler
- chunky crayons
- newsprint paper
- fat pencils
- wide-tip, water-soluble markers
- fat paint brushes and water

For the older toddler
- watercolor paints
- water-soluble markers
- glue sticks
- construction paper
- child-sized scissors
- hole punch
- pencils and ink pens
- scrap paper of all colors

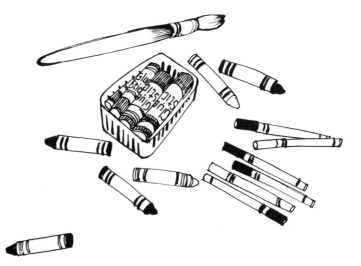

There is great delight for your child in drawing with crayons, pencils, and markers. She may spend hours on this activity, producing reams of drawings. Be sure to keep the emphasis on the creating, not on the objects created. What she produces doesn't have to be "something" and probably isn't, in her mind.

Say things like, "I can see that you like doing that. Look at the way your arm moves back and forth with your crayon." Or, "You are filling up the whole paper with your red crayon." Or, "You must be strong! Look at how dark that pencil mark is. You are using your muscles to press the pencil onto the paper." Your toddler's interest is in using the tools and seeing how her body works.

Creative ways with watercolor

To introduce toddlers to watercolors, put just a little water in the bottom of a plastic margarine tub. Add a drop of food color. Let your child paint on paper towels, napkins, or other absorbent paper. Be sure to put a layer of newspaper down first to catch spills.

Your child can use watercolor markers on paper towels. She will soon discover that when she leaves the pen on the towel, the color spreads out from where the pen tip is. Try the watercolor markers on coffee filters, too.

Tip: If you have a dishwasher, it can take on an additional role as art center. On those days when you know you can't handle spills and mess, open the dishwasher door, pull up your child's chair, and let her use the door as her table for painting. If spills happen, the paint will go into the dishwasher and not onto the floor. Her art work can dry on the dish rack.

Free or inexpensive art materials

You can get great art paper of all colors at your local copy center. Take a box with you and go ask for some of their recycled paper. Your local newspaper may have newsprint roll-ends available free or at a low price. These may come in different widths.

You can ask stores that offer gift wrapping service to save gift wrap scraps and ribbon pieces for your child. He will enjoy using these items for glue projects, as well as painting and coloring on them.

Picture framing shops will usually let you take small pieces of matboard that would otherwise go into their recycling bins.

Matboard makes a wonderful drawing material for young toddlers because it is so sturdy. It absorbs paint well, too. Matboard is also strong enough to be a good base for projects using paste. It will support the weight of a lot of stuff piled and pasted on it.

If you know people who have computers, ask them to save long sheets of computer paper. Just turn the printed side over and your toddler has space for miles of art.

Look for art materials at your grocery store. Buy rolls of shelf paper on sale for easel painting. Paper lunch sacks are fun for drawing or pasting activities, or for puppets. What about that paper sack you brought all your groceries home in? Let your child decorate the bag for a costume. Cut the bag up the front and then cut a round hole in the bottom of the bag to fit around his neck. Cut out arm holes in the sides. When he tires of his costume, recycle it!

Paste for toddlers

Toddlers use lots of supplies when they create. You will want to have on hand a batch of homemade paper (and cardboard) paste. This costs very little compared to store-bought paste and glue.

Recipe for paper paste

1/3 cup wheat flour (not self-rising)

2 tablespoons sugar

1 cup water

Mix flour and sugar in a saucepan. Add water slowly, stirring constantly. Stir until lumps are gone. Cook over low heat until the mixture is clear, stirring constantly. Store paste in a covered container for several weeks. No need to refrigerate.

Let's Play Ball

Children develop both small and large muscle control while playing ball. They also develop good eye-hand coordination. For the youngest toddlers, use large, lightweight balls like beach balls. As your toddler gets bigger and more coordinated, the balls can get smaller.

Some different kinds of balls for toddlers are sponge, tennis, rubber (as large as tennis balls), inflatable, soccer, football, basketball, crocheted, whiffle, beach, sock, and so on. The sheer variety means loads of enjoyment for your toddler.

Tip: To make a sock ball, cut off the toe part of the sock about five inches from the toe. Stuff it with the cut-off sock. Gather up the open edge of the stuffed toe and sew it closed. You can make sock balls from old nylons in the same way, stuffing them with soft, cotton fabric.

Roll the ball to me

Sit with your child on the floor and make a V-shape with your legs. Have your child sit with her feet out, touching your feet. Now you have a closed-in space for a ball game. Roll the ball to your child and say, "Here comes the ball. Can you roll it back to me?" Take turns until she tires of the game.

Ball in the box

Get a box bigger than the ball you want to use for this game. Cut a hole in the bottom of the box. Put the ball in the box and tip the box back and forth until the ball falls out. Your child will be delighted and surprised! Let her try to tip out the ball. Once she can do that while watching the ball, put the lid on the box so she cannot see when the ball will fall out.

Catch the ball

As kids get older, they begin to throw the ball. Make sure your toddler aims down when she throws  the ball, instead of up. Show her how to bounce it. Teach her how to throw it underhanded, as well as overhanded. Put away all breakable items in the room, or play in a large, open space. It takes a lot of practice to gain control of a ball.

Be patient with your toddler and let her enjoy what she can do now.

Throwing "snowballs"

The bottom of a cardboard box makes a good ball-toss target. Your child will have many hours of entertainment learning to throw the ball into the box. You can also put the box upside down and she can practice throwing the ball at it. Draw a funny face on the box for her to aim at.

Feeding the animals

Draw an animal face on the bottom of the box, with an opening cut out for the animal's mouth. Lean the box slantwise against a wall and let your child toss the ball into the box to "feed the animal."

Funny-face ball toss

Decorate several paper plates with funny faces. Tape a long string or piece of yarn to one edge of the paper plates. Tape the other end of the yarn to the top of a doorway, so the plates hang down at about a child's eye level. Let your child toss wadded newspaper balls at the targets and watch the funny faces swing.

Pop bottle bowling

Here is a variation on bowling using recyclables. Put sand in the bottom of six to eight 2-liter-sized, plastic pop (soda) bottles. Replace the caps. Set the bottles up in two rows. Show your child how to roll the ball and knock over the bottles. A fairly large or heavy ball works best.

There are lots of other outdoor ball games you can play with your toddler. Try kicking a large ball, chasing a ball, playing catch (stand about four feet away from her to start) with a large, soft ball, etc.

Tip: Some children, especially those who wear glasses, may be afraid the ball will hit them in the face. Start by using a soft ball and throwing it gently to your child, aiming at her waist.

Active Games for Indoors

Children need to move. We have talked about dance as one way to use extra energy. There are many other ways to get the wiggles out indoors, on a rainy day or when you can't take your child outside. **Supervise your toddler carefully during active play.** Make sure the play space is safe. Remove any furniture or objects that might hurt your child if he falls or bumps into them. Your days will be more pleasant if your toddler has a chance to be active. He will be developing large muscle control. He will eat, sleep, and feel better.

Riding on an airplane

Get out a big cardboard box and let your toddler make an airplane out of it (with your help). Put a child-sized chair and small table inside the box. Now he is ready to take a trip. Let him eat his snack "on the airplane." He can move the box around the room for take-offs and landings.

A box can be any other kind of vehicle, too. Trains made of several boxes are especially fun. Suggest to your toddler that he take a trip and invite his stuffed animals and dolls to go with him. Pretend with him: "Going on an errand? See you later. Have a good trip and drive carefully. Don't forget to put the dolly's seat belt on!"

Bouncing baby

A crib mattress that is not being used to sleep on makes a fine "trampoline." Cover the mattress with a crib sheet and let your child bounce. It is amazing how long he will enjoy such an activity. Be sure there is nothing nearby to fall against. Bouncing is sheer joy for a toddler!

Tons of bubbles

Get out the bubble mix and let your child pop bubbles as you blow them. Suggest that he pop them with his feet as they hit the floor. Next, ask him if he can pop them with his hand, then his knee. This is a challenge for young toddlers because it requires coordination and balance. He may create his own imaginative methods for popping bubbles.

Animal pretend

Put on some music and pretend to be different animals. How does a kangaroo jump? How does a snake slither? How does a frog hop? How does a puppy wiggle?

Can your toddler walk like a gorilla, with her fists on the floor? Can she stretch like a cat? Go through some magazines with animal pictures for ideas. Let your toddler create sound effects to go with the movements of different animals.

Ladder stepping

Lay a short, straight ladder on the floor and show your child how she can step over the rungs. After this becomes easy for her, tape each end securely to empty milk cartons to raise the ladder off the floor a few inches. This creates a more challenging obstacle. She will develop concentration and coordination. Hold her hand at first if she needs help balancing as she steps over the rungs.

Over the mountain

Pile up soft pillows to create a mountain for your child to climb on. She will spend a lot of time climbing up and rolling down. Suggest that she move the pillows to the other side of the room and build her own mountain. If you live near mountains, tell her their names. She might name her mountain after the real ones.

Nature's Playground

When the sun is shining and it is a beautiful day, go outside. Celebrate the good weather. The outdoors is a huge and wonderful natural playground for young children. There are many things you can do. A few are listed here, and you will surely think of more.

Bird watching

In the spring, when the birds are busy, go for a walk. Tell your child, "Today, we are going to look for birds. Let's see how many we can see. Do you think we will see any flying? Do you think we will see any getting a worm?" As you walk, point out the birds to her. Stop and listen to the sounds the birds make. Your child gains an appreciation for the birds' movements and songs. She is practicing listening skills, too.

Consider putting in a homemade bird bath or bird feeder for many hours of entertainment during the summer or winter. The birds will appreciate the refreshing stop for water and a bath or for food when it is hard to find. Your child will be able to see birds close up.

(Look, also, for squirrels, chipmunks, worms, insects, lizards, cats—whatever creatures live in your neighborhood.)

Listen to the sounds

Go for a walk around your neighborhood. Comment on things you hear. For example, say, "Oh, I think I hear an airplane. Does that sound like an airplane to you?" Point out the noises the wind makes, the cars rushing by on the street, the neighbor's lawn mower, dogs barking, sirens screaming, other people talking, etc. Soon your child will let you know what sounds he hears.

Yard "work"

Keep in mind how much toddlers like to copy the adults around them. If you are working in the yard, or helping with neighborhood clean-up, let your toddler help dig, rake, sweep, haul, and plant. A cardboard box with a short rope to pull it makes a good container for hauling small amounts of dirt, leaves, trash, and so on.

Walking in the rain

On a rainy day you can share a wonderful activity with your child. Put your rain boots and slickers on and go outside! If the weather is warm, go out in swimsuits. Give your child the great experience of a walk in the rain. Let him feel the raindrops on his cheeks. Stop to watch the water swirl around the curb. Point out the rings that the raindrops make as they land in a puddle. Ask him, "Do you think the birds will take a bath in the puddle when the rain stops? See how green the leaves look when they are wet? I wonder if there will be a rainbow today?" **Safety note:** Do not go out in thunder storms.

Buckets of fun

Bring a pail of water and a house-painting brush outside. Let your child "paint" the side of your house, the fence, etc. This activity is popular for all children. As she gets older, she may notice that the water dries up or evaporates. You can help her understand about evaporation. She'll enjoy saying such a large word, too.

Cooking with a Toddler Chef

Your toddler may go through a stage when he is too busy exploring to take time to eat. He needs to eat regular, well-balanced meals to maintain his high activity level. Your challenge is to think of ways to get food into him. You want to remain calm, and be patient and enthusiastic about his interest in exploring. Here are some ideas to keep mealtime a positive experience for you both.

Toddlers are developing new taste buds and may be sensitive to strong flavors. Keep foods simple and not too spicy. Their mouths are sensitive to hot temperatures. Dish up your child's plate first so it has time to cool before you serve it to him. Don't overwhelm your child by filling his plate with food. Serve one or two tablespoons of each item and offer seconds.

One way to encourage interest in mealtime is to let your child help prepare the meal. Teach him to wash his hands before handling food or cooking and eating utensils. In addition to helping set the table, he can do many "cooking" activities:

Pouring. Let your child pour the milk or water into batter for muffins, cakes, etc.

Stirring. He can stir the batter with a wooden spoon. Make sure that you use a plastic mixing bowl and that the work surface is easily cleaned up.

Shaking. He can help mix the salad dressing. Use a tightly closed plastic container to shake the ingredients in.

Tip: You can show him how to make fresh butter by shaking heavy whipping cream in a container. It takes a while to get butter, but if your child has patience, he will be rewarded. Point out the changes taking place in the mixture—from thick, creamy liquid to something that produces a clunking sound in the container, to a watery liquid and a clump of . . . yes, it's butter! Use the butter on your toddler's bread at dinner.

Spreading. He can use a butter knife (which is not sharp) to spread butter, soft cream cheese, peanut butter, tuna salad and other spreadable items onto bread, bagels, pita, crackers, tortillas, etc.

Tearing. Think of all the pages from magazines your child has ripped. He can put this skill to use at dinnertime. Give your child the head of lettuce and let him rip to his heart's content. It's quite an accomplishment to fill a bowl with wonderful green lettuce for the salad.

As your child gets older, you can introduce other utensils to him. Let him try his hand at a whisk, spatula, strainer, or rolling pin. He will need a lot of practice before he can accomplish a task without making a mess. He is still a success, however, because his job at this age is to practice using the utensils.

Think of other ways you can involve your child in helping with food preparation. All of the things listed here are safe, as they are not actually cooking. But children are involved and feel a great sense of accomplishment.

Safety note: Make sure that your child stands or sits on a stable surface, and has a stable place to work. For a nifty work area, place your child in his high chair pushed up to the counter. Pull out a breadboard so that he has his own work space.

Be sure to check with parents before you offer food to a child other than your own.

Gifts for Toddlers

You can provide your toddler, or a friend's toddler, with wonderful birthday gifts that are made or gathered with care and thoughtfulness. These gifts are the most appreciated because they provide hours of play. All are inexpensive, or cost nothing, to make. Sometimes the most interesting gift for a toddler is you time.

Playdough packages

Playdough packages can be personalized for the child receiving the gift. (See page 47 for playdough recipe.) If your child loves bears, make a batch of playdough scented with cinnamon. Put it together with bear cookie cutters and a copy of *The Three Bears* in a basket like the one Goldilocks might have used. If he enjoys building things, put a batch of playdough in a plastic container. Add a plastic hammer and some plastic or wooden pegs. Now your builder can construct a playdough structure.

A batch of playdough with sparkling confetti in it goes well with star cookie cutters. Include a story book with a nighttime theme. Some good ones are *A Child's Good Night Book* by Margaret Wise Brown, *Grandfather Twilight* by Barbara Berger, and *Baby Night Owl* by Leslie McGuire.

Paper dolls

Paper dolls are not a new toy, but this version offers a sturdier model than the ones our grandparents played with.

From sturdy cardboard or tagboard (get this at an office supply or art store), cut two body shapes. Draw a face and hair on each with felt markers or crayons. Using lighter weight paper cut out clothes for the dolls to wear. Color or paint them, and glue buttons or trim onto them. You can make underwear and glue it directly onto the dolls. Personalize the dolls by using the birthday child's eye and hair color for one doll and another child's coloring for the other doll. If the gift is for your child, make the other doll look like one of his favorite playmates.

Show the children how to dress and undress the dolls. Show them how to play make-believe with the dolls, imitating common experiences—eating dinner, playing with toys, going for a walk, etc. When children are older, they will be able to make up all kinds of imaginative adventures for their paper dolls.

Tape supply

Taping things keeps children busy for many hours. Buy a selection of tape rolls, from magic mending tape to colored masking tape. If you look around, you may be able to find mirrored tape or patterned tape. Add construction paper to the package to complete this dandy gift.

Time and attention

Give the gift of yourself to your child or a little friend. Write a gift certificate, inviting the child to go with you to a playground, to the lake to feed the ducks, or to your own home for story reading, singing, or creative art. Plan to serve the toddler's favorite snack on any of these occasions. You may think of other places where you can take a toddler.

The visit should not be longer than the child has energy for. It should take place at a time of day when the child is rested. Remember that the best gift we can give to anyone, especially our children, is our time.

Penny jar

Use a two-liter pop (soda) bottle to collect all the loose change you have in the bottom of your purse or wallet each week. Soon you'll have enough for a splurge purchase for a toddler. Here are a few suggestions for those extra few dollars you collect in this convenient way:

- Take your toddler to a used-book store and let him pick out a book.
- Visit a fabric store to buy a yard of chiffon to make a soft, billowy parachute. Or cut up the fabric to make several scarves.
- Stop at a garage or yard sale, or the thrift store, and let him select a used toy. Check to be sure the toy is safe and works right.
- Take a city bus ride anywhere. Stop along the way for a snack.

Contact paper fun

A great investment is a roll of contact paper, available at hardware or variety stores. It has a thousand uses. Here are just a few.

Peel back a foot-long section of contact paper. Tape it down, sticky side up, on a cardboard box. At first, just let your child feel what "sticky" is all about. As he tires of this activity, offer items for him to stick onto the contact paper. Small pieces of tissue or other paper, plastic bottle tops, ribbon, yarn, etc. are useful. Save these items instead of throwing them away. After some days, when the paper is no longer sticky, let your child pull off the items and put them in a container to save for another contact paper game.

Cut a hole in a piece of cardboard. Stick contact paper over the hole. Give your child scraps of many kinds of paper to create a beautiful work of art framed by the cardboard.

Make a photo album using extra photos of family, friends, or special places. Put contact paper over the pictures. Of course, you can't peel the contact paper off again, so use only photos you can spare.

Protect books you and your child put together with contact paper. By covering the pages, sticky fingers won't ruin the pictures. The pages will be sturdier and harder to rip. Use contact paper to cover the pictures you have placed on milk carton cubes.

Let your child stick beautiful fall leaves onto a sheet of contact paper. Cover with another piece of contact paper. Pat out the bubbles and together you have made a fall collage.

You will discover many other uses for this interesting, sticky paper. It's a wonderful material for lots of inexpensive play for toddlers.

Play Group Planning

Handling a group of toddlers is a real challenge! Maybe you are having a play group at your house, doing child care for a bunch of toddlers, or giving a birthday party. Whatever the occasion, you need an action plan. Action is what you will have, so it might as well be organized. The five group activities included here are organized around themes that small children like a lot. You will be able to think of others that your toddler especially likes.

There are several ways children express themselves and learn through play. Try to include one activity from each of these major categories in whatever theme you choose.

- **Art:** Making a mess; creating for the fun of it
- **Manipulatives:** Something for busy hands to do
- **Sensory:** Feeling different things
- **Cooking:** Making something delicious to eat
- **Social:** Stories, games, and songs
  (All books listed in the activities can be checked out of your public library.)

How to avoid problems

Toddlers are just starting to learn about ownership. A toddler may see a toy like hers and think it is hers. She can hold tight to something and become upset because another toddler looks at it. When another child picks up a toy, the owner may suddenly be overcome with the need to have it—NOW! Here are a few things you can do to reduce problems over possessions:

- Let your child know friends will be coming over to play. Wait to tell her until about one half hour before the arrival, so she doesn't get overexcited just thinking about the visit.
- Ask your child if there are any special toys she wants to put away before the guests arrive. Help her put the items away. Remind her that she will get them back after

the children leave. (Some items are just too precious to share. There is no need to force her to try.)

LET CHILD KNOW FRIENDS ARE COMING OVER TO PLAY. PUTTING SPECIAL TOYS AWAY IS OKAY.

- Ask parents to bring toys for their children. Then your child is not "giving up" all her toys to the whole group.
- Give equal attention to each child attending play group, so all feel special and recognized. Let each child have his or her time in the spotlight.
- Provide activities where children work on something together. Let each child contribute to the whole. Comment on their efforts. Say, "Look what you all made together." Avoid pointing out the efforts of any one child. Instead, say that each child added his or her part to make one beautiful thing. Children at this age enjoy the process of making things, not what those things become. Let parents know ahead of time that they can ask what their child **did,** instead of what he or she made.
- Toddlers can become overexcited or tired. Provide a corner with books and pillows for resting. Sometimes a short change of scene will calm a child and prepare him or her to rejoin the group.
- Ask parents if their children have any food restrictions. And now let the fun begin!

Get-Acquainted Games

Set the stage for children to play and work happily together. Give them time to get to know each other the first time they meet. Offer lots of "community" activities.

Some children don't like to be the center of attention, at least not at first. Focus more attention on the group, rather than on one child. When you call to invite a child, ask parents to tell you something wonderful about their child. Tell this news as you welcome each child to the group. If the child is willing, you can clap for her or him.

A necklace for Mom (or other important person)

Making something for someone else is a way of showing that we care. Children can share their skill at stringing macaroni, buttons, or sections of plastic straws to make necklaces for their mothers or someone else important to them (dads like homemade necklaces, too). Place a big container of "beads" on the floor or on a low table where all the children can reach. Give each child a white shoelace on which to string the "beads" of his or her choice. Be sure to put a big knot in one end of the shoelace, which can be removed later.

A house for us all

Working together, the children can construct a house for the whole group. They can use boxes, card tables, chairs, sheets, scarves, and whatever else you are willing to let them use. You can help out by taping cloth edges to furniture. Is the house big enough for you to fit inside with the toddlers? If so, ask them to invite you in to read a story together.

Skyscraper sandwich

This sandwich is so tall that it has to lie down flat or it will fall over! Slice a large loaf of French bread down the middle, so that you have two flat sides. Let the children "paint" the "walls" with peanut butter and jelly. Let them fill the "rooms" with banana and apple slices, raisins, and coconut. After you cut the sandwich into "floors," they can eat the whole "building." Toddlers love this game. It appeals to their budding sense of humor. **Safety note:** Be sure to ask parents about food restrictions before offering food to any child.

Billions of bubbles

Just imagine the fun and excitement of working up a mess of bubbles! Everybody can help. Put towels down on the floor for the toddlers to sit on. Fill dishpans with just a little water and lots of dish soap or make the recipe for billions of bubbles (see page 53). Place one pan in front of two or three children. Give the children wire whisks and other kitchen utensils to help them create mountains of bubbles. How tall can the mountains be before they fall over? Remind the parents to bring a change of clothes for the soon-to-be wet children.

Toddler chorus

It's time to sing a few songs together. Ask the children what their favorite songs are. Encourage them to help sing activity songs by doing the motions along with you. Sing activity songs in which everyone does the same thing: clap hands, jump high, touch toes, turn around, sit down, shake hands with another child, shake a leg, . . . The possibilities are as boundless as their energy! When they tire of this game, sit them down in a circle and read a couple of favorite stories to them. Show them the pictures as you go. Put as much expression into your voice as you can. Read slowly.

Teddy Bear Tea Party

Children love stuffed animals. A party with a theme involving a creature most, or all, of them own is always a hit. It even "bears" repeating, perhaps with other categories of stuffed animals (pets, farm animals, wild animals, etc.).

Invite each child to bring a teddy bear to the party. Plan to have a few extra bears, if possible, just in case someone forgets a bear or doesn't have one to bring. Start the party by having a "show and tell," in which each child shows off his or her teddy bear and tells the group about it. Some children may not want to speak. That's all right.

Remembering that children love the process of making things, be prepared for fun and mess as you do the following activities.

Teddy bear beds

Give each child a cardboard box to decorate with various sticky items—stickers, labels, sticky dots, pieces of contact paper, and tape. You can visit a fabric shop and ask for "discontinued sample boards of upholstery fabrics." Cut the sample pieces of fabric out of the books with scissors or pinking shears. Let each child choose a "blanket" for his or her teddy bear.

Teddy bear headbands

Children love to wear crowns. Cut a two-inch wide strip of heavy paper to fit around the child's head. Glue, staple, or tape it closed. Instead of crown points on the party hats, put bear ears. Headbands can be decorated with markers or crayons. The toddlers can also put sticky dots on them.

Cinnamon bear playdough

If you have enough time, let the children make a batch of playdough with your help. Mix two teaspoons of cinnamon with the other playdough ingredients (see page 47 for playdough recipe). Provide teddy bear cookie cutters and let the children play for a while.

Safety note: Before letting children mix the dough, make sure most of the cinnamon has been absorbed. Inhaling cinnamon "dust" is not pleasant. Also, this playdough smells good, but it doesn't taste good. One taste and a child will know!

Beary nice necklaces

Older toddlers can thread short pasta pieces onto shoelaces to make necklaces for their bears. Color the pasta ahead of time to make colorful "beads." Variation: use buttons and wooden or plastic beads instead of pasta.

Recipe for colored pasta

Mix together in a jar:

3 tablespoons rubbing alcohol

1 tablespoon food coloring

Add pasta to the jar, put on the lid, and shake. When the pasta are colored, pour them out on newspaper to dry. **Safety note:** Making colored pasta is an adult activity.

Teddy bear chefs

Let the children help make sandwiches for their tea party. They can spread cream cheese on sturdy crackers or small bagels. They can help set the table with paper plates, napkins, and cups. Of course, they get to eat the food, but their teddy bears can sit next to them and watch. **Safety note:** Be sure to ask parents about food restrictions before offering food to any child.

All-together time

Sing and do the motions to "Teddy Bear, Teddy Bear, Turn Around" before you settle everyone down to one or two great stories about teddy bears. These books are available in the public library. Some excellent choices are *Corduroy* by Don Freeman, *Jamberry* by Bruce Degen, *Where's My Teddy?* by Jez Albrough, and the Jesse Bear books by Nancy White Carlstrom.

Then, put "Teddy Bear Picnic" on the record player or cd player. The children will love dancing with their bears to the music.

If music is not available to you, line up the children and their bears for a parade around the house or yard. A drum adds exciting drama and noise to the parade.

I Love a Parade

Celebrate a special day—or make one up—by having a parade. You can entertain a group of children and the neighbors with this theme activity. Have each child bring a favorite riding toy. Possibilities include tricycles, wagons, big wheels, etc.

Face painting

What celebration would be complete without a lovely face decoration? Use face painting crayons or just watercolor pencils dipped in water to create great designs.

Safety note: Keep paint away from eyes. A cheek decoration is probably enough for a toddler. **Face painting should be done by an adult.**

Newspaper hats

These are easy to make and fun to decorate. You need a supply of newspapers and masking tape. Put two or three newspaper sheets together. Fold up the bottom edge three times. Each fold should be one to two inches wide. Place the newspaper around the child's head to measure. Remove the hat and put masking tape on the newspaper. You can make interesting shapes by cutting or taping the top of the hat into the form of horns, or feathers, or braids, etc. Children can decorate their hats with crayons, markers, and stickers.

Banners

Let children color or paint on white fabric, such as pieces of old sheet or diapers. When the paint is dry, tape the fabric to wooden dowels or sticks to make flags.

Fabulous floats

What would a parade be without floats? Let children tape crepe paper streamers onto their vehicles. For added excitement, tie some tin cans to the vehicles, too. Have someone lead the parade playing a drum made from a pot and a wooden spoon. With all the noise, excitement, and color, the neighbors will surely come out to see the parade go by. Invite them to join it.

Ice cream and confetti

Ice cream and parades go together. If you have a crank-type ice cream maker, let the children take turns cranking before the ice cream gets too hard. Another choice is to let children decorate ice cream sundaes with candy confetti. Serve small paper cups of water to go with the ice cream. **Safety note:** Be sure to check with parents before you offer food to any child.

All-together time

Everyone will have worked together to get this parade going. If possible, ask someone to videotape it, so that the children can watch themselves later.

After the parade, gather around and read *Parade* by Donald Crews.

Magical Fantasy Day

Even the youngest child loves to play a pretend game of kings and queens and castles. Bring those fairy tales to life. Ask each child to bring his or her own special cape today. These can be made easily from a colorful piece of fabric cut to wrap around the child's shoulders, trailing to the back of the knees, and fastened with a big safety pin under the chin. A bit of costume helps the children's imaginations run wild.

Magic wands

Cut star shapes from light-weight cardboard. To make a wand, tape a tongue depressor or other flat stick on one side of the star. Children can fill their star with shiny stickers and/or color it with gold and silver crayons. Tie some crepe paper streamers to the wand.

· CUT OUT STAR SHAPES FROM TAGBOARD.

· TAPE POPSICLE STICK ON STAR.

· CHILD CAN DECORATE WAND!

Royal crowns

Cut lengths of heavy paper long enough to go around a child's head. Each length should be about five inches wide. Children can design beautiful crowns by coloring with markers and crayons. Remind them that crowns often have jewels of different colors in them. Put each child's decorated crown around his or her head and tape to fit.

· PRECUT CROWN SHAPES FROM HEAVY PAPER.

· CHILD CAN PUT ON STICKERS AND SHINY THINGS.

· TAPE OR STAPLE CROWN TO FIT JUST RIGHT.

Build a castle

A large appliance box can be made into a castle for the children to live in. Place the box with the opening on top. Tape the flaps shut to form the roof. Cut some tall, skinny windows in two sides. Make a drawbridge by cutting a flap that opens from the top and lays flat on the floor (or ground). Tape heavy string to it so that a child can lower and raise the drawbridge from inside the castle.

Children can create castles for small toy people out of blocks. Some toy dinosaurs (dragons) will add a lot of fun and excitement. Inexpensive, plastic ones are available in toy stores. You can also use stuffed animals who are pretending to be dinosaurs.

Magic playdough

Make a batch of playdough before the party. (See recipe on page 47.) Add sparkling plastic (not metallic) confetti instead of food coloring. The playdough will be white, but will shine where light hits the confetti. Provide star cookie cutters for the children to make magic star cookies.

Royal dining

Finger gelatin is a tasty, colorful treat that can look like jewels. The children can pretend they are eating rubies, sapphires, emeralds, amethysts. To make finger gelatin, follow the directions on the box of flavored gelatin.

All-together now

Have a royal parade of queens, kings, princesses, and princes. Fairies, court jesters, knights, and dragons can join, too. Let the children dress up in their capes and carry their magic wands. Put some marching music on the record player or cd player. Sing "Puff, the Magic Dragon." Read *Drac and the Gremlin* by Allan Baillie.

Delightful Dinosaurs

Even the youngest children seem to have a fascination with dinosaurs. You can turn your backyard into the perfect Jurassic Park, complete with romping, stomping dinosaurs!

Dinosaur hats

Cut lengths of heavy paper long enough to go around a child's head. Each length should be about two inches wide. The color of the paper doesn't matter—even the ugliest color will do. Cut out and staple lots of spikes and a long, bumpy tail to each hat. Let the children color both sides and add stickers. Place the strip of paper around the child's head and tape closed.

Cardboard carnivores

Cut familiar dinosaur shapes from large pieces of cardboard. Have the children paint the shapes with paste (see page 77 for recipe). Then let them stick pieces of fabric, crumpled paper, bits of sandpaper, etc. to the shapes to create the dinosaurs' skin. Place the figures around the yard (or house) to set the scene.

- CUT 2 PIECES OF CONSTRUCTION PAPER WITH SPIKES

- CUT ONE BUMPY TAIL.

- LET CHILDREN COLOR THEM! ADD STICKERS.

- STAPLE TOGETHER.

- ROARRR!

Dinosaur eggs

The children can make eggs by stuffing lunch sacks with crumpled newspaper. Hold a bag open while a child stuffs in the newspaper, and then tape the bag shut. Squash the sack into an egg shape, round or oval. Let children paint the eggs with tempera paint. When the eggs are dry, hide them around the yard. Play hide-and-seek with the eggs.

Spiky dinosaurs

Now is the time to use up old playdough. Let the children mix all the colors together, until they get a good, "yucky" color. Give each child a piece of playdough to shape into a dinosaur. Offer them small wooden pegs or blunt-ended toothpicks to create spikes on the dinosaurs. Children love to put spikes in and take them out, over and over again.

Dinosaur habitat

Fill the bottom of a dishpan with sand, pebbles, and several larger stones. Add water. Let the children build volcanos and tar pits for the dinosaurs to live in. Remind them that many dinosaurs ate plants instead of each other. They may want to add tiny, leafy branches for food. Small plastic dinosaurs add a great deal to the fun. Inexpensive ones can be bought at department and toy stores.

Dinosaur lunch

Lots of dinosaurs liked to eat plants. Ask the children to think about what plants people eat. Let the children help make a vegetable salad that has parts of plant leaves, stems, and roots in it for snack. Even the most reluctant eater will try something he or she has helped prepare. Since dinosaurs laid eggs, how about deviled or hardboiled eggs to go with the salad? **Safety note:** Be sure you check with parents before you offer food to any child.

All-together now

Children love to romp and stomp, so let them be dinosaurs. Make up a movement activity, creating a story about the dinosaurs in your group. The children could begin by moving quickly to find food, stop and nibble on some grasses, then move slowly because they are so full. Keep the game simple. Add music for a special touch.

Change the words of "Going on a Bear Hunt" to fit a dinosaur hunt, ending in a cave. There the children find the dinosaur, and run back home.

Read *Whatever Happened to the Dinosaurs?* and *What if the Dinosaurs Came Back?* by Bernard Most.

Index

Order these books for quick ideas

Tools for Everyday Parenting Series
Illustrated. Paperback, $9.95 each; library binding, $18.95 each

These books are geared for new or frustrated parents. Fun to look at and fun to read, they present information in both words and cartoons. They are perfect for parents who may be busy with school, jobs, or other responsibilities and who have little time to read.

Magic Tools for Raising Kids, by Elizabeth Crary • Parenting young children is easier and more effective with a toolbox of useful, child-tested, positive tools. Learn what to do, how to do it, and what to say to make raising lovable, self-confident kids easier.
128 pages, ISBN 0-943990-77-7 paperback, 0-943990-78-5 library

365 Wacky, Wonderful Ways to Get Your Children to Do What You Want, by Elizabeth Crary • Young children share certain behaviors that are calculated to drive parents crazy. Here are hundreds of practical (and sometimes zany) ideas to help parents cope.
104 pages, ISBN 0-943990-79-3 paperback, 0-943990-80-7 library

More books and ordering information on next page

Order these books for quick ideas

More books on preceding page. **Paperback, $9.95 each; library binding $18.95 each**

Peekaboo and Other Games to Play with Your Baby, by Shari Steelsmith • Babies love games and this book is full of games they enjoy at different stages of development. All games help develop skills, are fun, and strengthen the bond between baby and parent.
120 pages, ISBN 0-943990-81-5 paperback, 0-943990-99-8 library

Joyful Play with Toddlers: Recipes for Fun with Odds and Ends, by Sandi Dexter • Toddlers at play are full of curiosity and daring. They need creative and safe ways to express themselves. Parents need lots of ideas for no-cost or low-cost toys, games, and activities.
128 pages, ISBN 1-884734-00-6 paperback, 1-884734-01-4 library

Taking Care of Me (So I Can Take Care of Others), by Barbara Carlson, Margaret Healy, Glo Wellman • By taking care of themselves, parents can take care of their children (and others) better. Learn how temperament, childhood experiences, basic needs, and goals affect parenting style.
104 pages, ISBN 1-884734-02-2 paperback, 1-884734-03-0 library

Ask for these books at your favorite bookstore, or call toll free 1-800-992-6657. VISA and MasterCard accepted with phone orders. Complete book catalog available on request.

Parenting Press, Inc., Dept. 502, P.O. Box 75267, Seattle, WA 98125
In Canada, call **Raincoast Books Distribution Co.,** 1-800-663-5714.
Prices subject to change without notice.